THE LITTLE BOOK OF
SPURS

Independent and Unofficial

FOURTH EDITION

EDITED BY
LOUIS MASSARELLA

**CARLTON
BOOKS**

First published by Carlton Books in 2004
Reprinted with updates in 2005, 2006, 2008, 2009
Second edition 2010, reprinted 2011, 2012
Third edition 2014
Fourth edition 2017
Reprinted in 2018

This book is not an officially licensed product of
Tottenham Hotspur Football Club

A CIP catalogue record of this book is available from the
British Library.

ISBN 978-1-78097-968-7

Printed in Dubai

CONTENTS

INTRODUCTION

One of the original Big Five clubs, no Premier League side has quite been able to inspire and frustrate in equal measure the way Tottenham Hotspur has. Brilliant success has been mixed with periods of mediocrity, yet big crowds and high expectations remain at White Hart Lane, in the hope that major trophies will come again, all won in the club's trademark style.

In this great collection of quotes, players past and present, famous fans and even more famous managers reveal why, for them, Lilywhite really is the colour. From the Glory, Glory days of the 1960s and the European and FA Cup successes of the 70s and 80s to the renaissance of recent years, there are soundbites here to satisfy every Spurs fan. Players such as Danny Blanchflower, Glenn Hoddle, Jurgen Klinsmann, Dele Alli and Harry Kane are all featured, along with a host of managers and chairmen, from Bill Nicholson and Terry Venables, to Alan Sugar and Mauricio Pochettino.

When it comes to Spurs, people are never short of an opinion and this book serves up quotes that are revealing and sometimes damning but always intriguing. A bit like Spurs themselves…

CHAPTER 1

GLORY, GLORY TOTTENHAM HOTSPUR

"The great fallacy is that the game is first and last about winning. It's nothing of the kind. The game is about glory. It's about doing things in style, with a flourish, about going out and beating the other lot, not waiting for them to die of boredom.**"**

DANNY BLANCHFLOWER

1972

"It is a matter of record that at White Hart Lane in 1930, the Spurs winger centred the old type of leather ball with such velocity on a wet Saturday afternoon, it struck the centre-forward, bounced off him and hit another player, resulting in both of them being carried off with concussion.**"**

VIN STANLEY
Football Shorts

"We'll win the Double for you this year – the League and the Cup.**"**

DANNY BLANCHFLOWER

Double-winning captain, to Spurs chairman Fred Bearman
on the eve of the 1960–61 season

“When I went to Spurs they were in the bottom four or five but started getting some decent players. Including myself.**”**

DAVE MACKAY

recalls modestly the turning point in the club's fortunes

“As far as the media were concerned, that Tottenham side were the bee's knees. They positively drooled over the men from White Hart Lane who could not put a boot wrong… Tottenham played with a style and a swagger that was to define their character over the years to come.**”**

ALEX FYNN and **OLIVIA BLAIR**
The Great Divide, *2000*

❝I did not enjoy dancing around, waving trophies in the air. I'm sure he didn't like it either. His comments regarding success were always cold… I was embarrassed by the boasting around us but I escaped it with humour. He gruffed his way out of it. Our satisfaction was in doing the job.**❞**

DANNY BLANCHFLOWER

on Bill Nicholson, 1972

"Big Nick always wanted us to win with style and entertain the fans. If we won a game and we'd played badly, he was disappointed. **"**

CLIFF JONES

2001

“ Than the famous Spurs there is probably no more famous club in the whole of England. Did they not recover the Association Cup for the South? Did they not play pretty and effective football? Are they not scrupulously fair? Are they not perfectly managed? **”**

WILLIAM PICKFORD and **ALFRED GIBSON**

authors, Association Football and the Men Who Made It, *1906*

❝When I went to Tottenham I was
really in love with the game. After six months,
I was ready for a transfer.**❞**

ALAN MULLERY

on the troubled start to his Spurs career, 1972

❝ When we had been there as players, two bad games and the fans were on your back; three bad games and they were rocking your car, trying to turn it over. **❞**

ALAN MULLERY

1972

❝The biggest regret of my whole football career was leaving White Hart Lane in 1970… My interest in football weakened after that. I was heartbroken.**❞**

JIMMY GREAVES

" We couldn't believe Bill had done it. We were gobsmacked. Jimmy was still a great player. **"**

ALAN MULLERY

on the departure of Spurs' greatest striker, 1972

❝Intelligence doesn't make you a good footballer. Oxford and Cambridge would have the best sides if that were true. It's a football brain that matters and that doesn't usually go with an academic brain. I prefer players not to be too good or too clever at other things. It means they concentrate on football.**❞**

BILL NICHOLSON
1970

❝I have no doubt whatsoever that Spurs are one of the biggest clubs in the land.**❞**

SAM HAMMAM

November 2000

"Spurs were like West Ham used to be, all fancy flicks and sweet sherry.**"**

PHIL SPROSON

Port Vale defender, after scoring against Spurs in
their FA Cup defeat to Vale, 1988

" One of my big tasks here is to keep the mediocrity away. Tottenham in the last few years have signed mediocre players. **"**

DAVID PLEAT

1998, on being appointed Director of Football

"We like a tackle at Tottenham.
We're not pansies, you know.**"**

DAVID PLEAT

caretaker manager, after a win at Derby, and 48 hours before George
Graham took over as manager, 1988

" Man in the raincoat's blue-and-white army. **"**

Chant by **SPURS FANS**
reluctant to use the former Arsenal manager's name, 1999

❝ I know Tottenham are not among the biggest clubs in England, but they are considered a very good club to play for, a nice place to play. **❞**

RIVALDO

2003

"We've had everyone.
Managers, agents, mothers, fathers,
dustmen, cleaners applying.**"**

DAVID PLEAT

on the search for Hoddle's successor, 2003

❝I was sitting just a few feet away from David Pleat at the World Cup. He's a nice fellow, but the man is mad: certifiably, eye-spinningly mad.**❞**

DANNY KELLY

co-host with Danny Baker, discussing Tottenham's Director of Football on a Talk Radio football phone-in, 1998

❝I wouldn't know what a long-ball team was. We pass the ball to death.**❞**

HARRY REDKNAPP

responds to criticism from Aston Villa keeper, Brad Freidel

CHAPTER 2

HEROES OF THE SHIRT

"Even the tea lady was told that she couldn't get the milk for the canteen delivered any more and that she had to get it from the supermarket herself on the way in. That was a complete joke.**"**

STEVE PERRYMAN

on the club's financial situation when he left Spurs in 1986

❝It doesn't matter who is getting on the scoresheet or who is setting up the goals as long as we're getting three points. **❞**

Midfielder **DELE ALLI**

2016

“Darren Anderton has had so many X-rays that he got radiation sickness.**”**

ALAN SUGAR

1997

"I'm 58 and I think even I've played more football than Anderton over the past two years. If the Black Death ever swept through London again, I would not even want to be in the next street to him because you can be sure he would get it. **"**

JIMMY GREAVES

1998

"Whenever I break down with injury, it's always 'Sicknote'. People read it and think it's funny. I've been out on the street, just walking along, and they shout, 'Sicknote!' It's not nice.**"**

DARREN ANDERTON

1998

" There are days when you think about it more than others and I even find myself talking to my leg, saying, 'Please don't let me down again.' **"**

JAMIE REDKNAPP

2002

" If things go according to plan I won't need to move to a bigger club because Tottenham will be big enough… If we add to the squad we can challenge for the championship in a year or two's time. **"**

LES FERDINAND

1997

We feel confident in our style of play, but in football things can change very quickly if you don't hvae the right behaviour and attitude. We have to continue working hard as we always have.

Club captain **HUGO LLORIS**

2017

“If someone wants to give
you a bum steer on who we're after, then so
be it. If you want to know, ask me, because
I have a list of players we want and Robbie
Keane isn't on it. **”**

GLENN HODDLE

*Tottenham manager, shortly before paying
Leeds United £7million for Robbie Keane*

"When you are a person of a certain age, with a certain intelligence, like he is, then why, if you are the manager, would you be jealous of someone who is playing well and is loved by the fans?**"**

DAVID GINOLA

on George Graham, 2000

41

"Graham would always give me hassle. I knew he wasn't a big fan of mine, but he should have respected what I could do. He would try to put me down in front of other players. Even if I had been the best on the pitch, he would point to me and say, 'I expect more from you.' He never did that to anyone else.**"**

DAVID GINOLA

on George Graham, 2000

"I loved the way Teddy Sheringham played, especially his movement. He was a real idol of mine growing up at the Lane and I've really tried to model myself on him.**"**

HARRY KANE

on his Tottenham hero, 2014

"He is one of the best strikers in the world.**"**

Manager **MAURICIO POCHETTINO**

on Harry Kane, 2016

" I was so upset – I felt like my life had been hit by a train. **"**

LUKA MODRIC

mistakes a fractured fibula for a horrific rail accident

" Even early on this season, when I hadn't scored for a few games, I was getting some criticism, so to then go on and win the Golden Boot shows I've had a great season. **"**

HARRY KANE

2015–16 Premier League top scorer

❝We played so well that the Liverpool fans applauded us off the pitch, having seen their team go out of the competition. That was special. **❞**

TEDDY SHERINGHAM

2002, on Spurs' victory at Anfield in the 1995 FA Cup quarter-final

" At the end of my 1994–95 season with Tottenham Hotspur, I got many letters and calls from teachers. They told me that the German language was becoming increasingly popular at schools. That, I think, is even better than successes on the pitch. **"**

JURGEN KLINSMANN

2002

"Because we've got Ledley at the back
(SOMETIMES!)
We've got Ledley at the back (SOMETIMES!)
We've got Ledley
We've got Ledley
We've got Ledley (SOMETIMES!)**"**

SPURS FANS

update an old classic for their dodgy-kneed skipper

❝ Steffen is only 20 and earns too much money for a boy of his age. **❞**

BENTE IVERSEN

the Spurs striker's mother, on her son's
£10,000-a-week wages, 1997

"He gets the little sniff type of goals.**"**

GLENN HODDLE

on Steffen Iversen, 2002

❝I don't drink or smoke and I've never touched drugs. All I wanted to do was be a footballer. A lot I used to play with have ended up in prison. It's very sad.❞

JERMAIN DEFOE

explains the straight and narrow route he took to the top

"Boom, boom, boom – everybody say Bale – BALE."

After a sizzling run of games, the **SPURS FANS**
finally welcome Gareth Bale as one of their own with an adaptation
of The Outhere Brothers' seminal early-1990s anthem

If you want to play with the big boys,
you have to play like the big boys.
Spurs don't. **"**

Ex-midfielder **EDGAR DAVIDS**

on why Spurs are still nearly men, December 2009

"He wasn't born, he was chiselled out of an oak tree.**"**

ALAN GREEN

BBC Radio Five Live commentator, praising Tom Huddlestone during Spurs's game against Manchester United in September 2007

" He's a good player. I think he's what we need. He's a good lad, great attitude. He's a good character, a fantastic person, a proper family man, a real good pro. He'll be great around the place for us. **"**

HARRY REDKNAPP

sings Scott Parker's praises, August 2011

"The Wolf of White Hart Lane."

SPURS FANS RIFF

on The Wolf of Wall Street *movie in praise of Emmanuel Adebayor, February 2014*

If you give confidence to someone like Ade, he will repay you so much more. He will give you the best.

YOUNES KABOUL

on Emmanuel Adebayor, February 2014

❝What he did in Milan, that wasn't a shock. I watched him do that every day in training – absolutely murder people and score goals. He was doing that week in, week out ripping teams to pieces, running down the left-hand touch line 50 yards, crossing balls for people to score, weighing in with quite a few goals as well.**❞**

HARRY REDKNAPP

is unsurprised by Gareth Bale's hat trick against Inter at the San Siro, October 2010

> **"**I was never too much into school. I liked lunchtimes and breaks, but nah, I hated sitting at a desk. I was always looking out of the window, looking at my watch, thinking about when I could play football.**"**

GARETH BALE

"I'm not afraid to go abroad.
If the time comes and a team that's right
comes in for me, then I'll look at it seriously.
I'll see what happens.**"**

GARETH BALE

hints he wants to leave Spurs, December 2012

"What he can achieve is scary. He has everything – he's six feet, can head it, has a great left foot and great touch.**"**

HARRY REDKNAPP

assesses Gareth Bale's future

"The kid is a bit confused at
the moment and it's not been easy for him.
I'd be telling you lies if I said he's happy
and he doesn't want to go and play for
whoever wants him.**"**

HARRY REDKNAPP

on an unsettled Luca Modric, July 2011

❝I think it was the right time for me to go, but I will always be thankful to Tottenham for everything they did for me. I became a better player there and they pushed me to this level where I am at the moment. I will always be a fan, I follow them a lot when I can.**❞**

LUCA MODRIC

looks back on his Spurs career, February 2014

“Mentally, we're strong enough. Maybe we're one of the best teams mentally because we support each other all the time.**”**

JAN VERTONGHEN

assesses the Spurs team, February 2014

❝This is a sensational challenge for me. I promise the fans hard work and I hope they will give me their full support in return.**❞**

ROBERTO SOLDADO

signing for Spurs, August 2013

❝I don't know what he looks like. I don't know him. I don't follow this kind of news. It's like two or three years ago, Rafael van der Vaart was there in training one day… I don't understand people who don't understand me [not showing an interest in football]. Most people don't go back home with their job and it's the same for me.**❞**

BENOIT ASSOU-EKOTTO

has no idea who his new team-mate Paulinho is, July 2013

“Eccentric, yes of course you can be, absolutely, but to be a top goalkeeper you can't be thick. **”**

BRAD FREIEDEL

tells it like it is, January 2014

❝Mentality is a big thing. We've been through the good experiences and also the bad experiences. We've experienced missing out on the final day last year. [Those experiences] can help you when you're under a bit of pressure.❞

MICHAEL DAWSON

Spurs captain, 2014

CHAPTER 3

BEAT YOUR NEIGHBOURS

❝I always felt there was a special role for Spurs; they were glam. They were great at attacking but they couldn't really defend. But you really didn't care, and you could feel special about them.**❞**

HARRY LANSDOWN

Arsenal fan, 1996

❝At White Hart Lane, the two teams were going down the tunnel and I felt this tugging from behind. As I was about to step onto the pitch with 30,000 people watching, Gazza was trying to pull my shorts down. Luckily, they were tied firmly, or I would have made my entrance with my kecks around my ankles.**❞**

DAVID SEAMAN

2000

73

"I have found Alan Sugar to be one of the least charming people I have ever come across. **"**

PETER HILL-WOOD

Arsenal Chairman, 1997

❝I do hate Arsenal. With a passion. No money in the world would ever tempt me to play for them.**❞**

TEDDY SHERINGHAM

Spurs striker and supporter, 1996

❝I used to dread losing
to Spurs, especially when a big England
game followed soon afterwards. The reason
was simple: I shared a room with Glenn
Hoddle, and he wouldn't miss a chance to
wind me up about it.**❞**

KENNY SANSOM
Arsenal and England full-back, 1996

"It doesn't matter what you do, just make sure you beat Arsenal."

SPURS FAN

to Terry Venables, on his appointment as manager, 1987

❝A season in which Spurs finished second in the League would be counted as a triumph, unless Arsenal finished first, in which case it would instantly become a disaster.**❞**

TERRY VENABLES

1994

“How am I betraying Spurs? I go to see Spurs win and Arsenal get stuffed. **”**

HUNTER DAVIES

who has a season ticket for both north London sides, 1998

❝What a nightmare. I'm a Tottenham fan
and I get cuffed to you.**❞**

FELLOW PRISONER

to Tony Adams on the night the latter was
arrested for drink-driving, 1998

" He hasn't stopped giving me stick since. He's always at it, but I say that's the only one he's scored against me. **"**

DAVID SEAMAN

on Gazza's free-kick in the 1991 FA Cup semi-final

“ Na-yim, from the halfway line,
Na-yim, from the halfway line. **”**

SPURS FANS

mock David Seaman after the ex-Spurs midfielder scored a freak
winner for Real Zaragoza against Arsenal in the 1995 European Cup-
Winners' Cup Final

82

❝ The Spurs fans loved it of course. They still remind me of it when we play them and the goal was the inspiration for their fanzine – *One Flew Over Seaman's Head*. **❞**

DAVID SEAMAN

2000

"The day I arrived in England I first went to White Hart Lane. I think I had a meeting with Mr Sugar or his assistant. I saw two people and they made me an offer, and two hours later they ordered me a black cab, it was pre-paid… and I went to see Arsène Wenger at his place. When I arrived he was with David Dein, and two hours later I had given my word to Arsenal.**"**

EMMANUEL PETIT

the one that got away

**I've learned never to say never.
Then again, I think I can safely say
I wouldn't join Tottenham!**

PATRICK VIEIRA

2004

❝I did really well to hold myself back. I really don't think he realises how strong I am, otherwise he wouldn't approach me with headbutts and everything.❞

MARTIN JOL

after a touchline confrontation with Arsène Wenger following the April 2006 Spurs–Arsenal match.

❝I grew up in a Tottenham-supporting area and most of my mates follow Spurs. They used to give me all sorts of stick when I played for Arsenal.**❞**

New signing, **DAVID BENTLEY**
looks forward to finally getting his friends off his back, July 2008

CHAPTER 4

IN THE BOARDROOM

"We have no desire just to be a football club. That is not the basis for success.**"**

PAUL BOBROFF

Chairman of Tottenham Hotspur plc, 1983

❝I like a challenge. If I'd been a woman, I would have been pregnant all the time because I can't say no.**❞**

ROBERT MAXWELL

on his interest in saving cash-strapped Spurs, 1990

❝Robert Maxwell's record is exemplary… He has always been prepared to invest heavily in football at a time when others are turning their backs on the game. Some people seem to doubt him, but they don't know the man.**❞**

IRVING SCHOLAR

Tottenham Chairman, 1990

❝I know more about schmaltz herring than I do about football. **❞**

ALAN SUGAR

to outgoing chairman Irving Scholar, before taking over at Spurs, 1991

❝He'd said that he bought
Spurs on 'a whim' after he and his family had
watched them win the 1991 FA Cup final.
If he'd known what he was in for in the
following ten years, he said, he would never
have done it. **❞**

RODNEY MARSH

on Alan Sugar, 2001

"If I fail, I'll stand up and be counted –
let some other brain surgeon take over.**"**

ALAN SUGAR

Tottenham Chairman, 1996

"When I took over, football was not fashionable. Going into the bank and asking for money was like asking a rabbi to eat a bacon sandwich. Now the banks are queuing up to lend.**"**

ALAN SUGAR

Tottenham Chairman, 1997

❝There's a limit to the thickness of the skin of the rhino. I want a goal at the end of the rainbow, or at least to be appreciated. What I won't accept is more abuse. I've been branded a cold, cynical individual with no knowledge of football and no interest in the club's heritage or traditions.**❞**

ALAN SUGAR

after protests against him by Spurs fans, 1998

❝I personally believe Spurs are very lucky to have someone like him. ❞

SAM HAMMAM

on Alan Sugar, 2000

❝[Alan] Sugar was hell bent on imposing his will on other people's lives and careers without giving a second thought to their true views or feelings. There were only two sides to an argument with Sugar – his and the wrong one.**❞**

TEDDY SHERINGHAM

1998

"We will not be pushed around by a bunch of north London yobbos."

RUPERT LOWE

Southampton Chairman, shortly before his
manager Glenn Hoddle left for Spurs

❝If Alan Sugar thinks he can just walk in and take West Bromwich Albion's manager, I'll be down that motorway in my car like an Exocet to blow up his bloody computers.**❞**

Baggies' Chairman, **TREVOR SUMMERS**
*on Tottenham's interest in Ossie Ardiles, just before he
left the Hawthorns for White Hart Lane*

"If he put a mask on, called himself Geraldo Francisco, and came back here tomorrow, things would turn around immediately. **"**

ALAN SUGAR

Tottenham Chairman, on Gerry Francis's resignation, 1997

"Harry will always be
welcome at the Lane.**"**

No hard feelings from Chairman **DANIEL LEVY**
despite sacking Harry Redknapp, June 2012

CHAPTER 5

GAFFER CHATTER

There used to be a football club over there.

KEITH BURKINSHAW

departs as manager in 1984 with a swipe
at the club's new owners

❝When you finish playing football, young man, which is going to be very soon, I feel, you'll make a very good security guard.❞

DAVID PLEAT

to 17-year-old Neil Ruddock, 1986

❝ The expectations of Spurs fans are always high, and if the 'Glory, Glory Days' are long gone, Tottenham fans still presume the team will play Glory, Glory football. **❞**

TERRY VENABLES

1994

❝It was definitely the hardest job I had ever had to do, and in the early months, I often shook my head at the scale of the task facing me, and thought to myself: 'How the hell do I do this?'**❞**

TERRY VENABLES

1994

❝When Gazza came to the Spurs training ground for the first time, he got the ball, went round eight players as if they were not there and then smashed the ball into the net. Just to see him play like that made the hair stand up on the back of your neck. Everybody stood there and applauded him.**❞**

TERRY VENABLES

1994

❝Tottenham without Terry is like Westminster without Big Ben.**❞**

PAUL GASCOIGNE's

reaction to Terry Venables' sacking by Alan Sugar, 1993

"Ask any Tottenham fan today about the team Terry was building and they will tell you it was the best they'd had for years and would have gone on to challenge for major honours in the next year or two.**"**

NEIL RUDDOCK

1999, on Terry Venables' departure

❝Part of his managerial reputation was built on the strength of his Tottenham side beating my lot from Nottingham in the 1991 FA Cup Final.**❞**

BRIAN CLOUGH

on Terry Venables, 2002

❝At least all the aggravation will keep me slim.❞

GEORGE GRAHAM

on encountering fan hostility at Tottenham
because of his Arsenal background, 1999

❝He's been a problem and if Aaron [Lennon] doesn't get injured, he probably doesn't play. I played Niko [Kranjcar] at first, because I didn't really feel at that time David deserved to play in all honesty. I suppose other managers probably wouldn't have had the patience that I've shown with him. Everyone's different and I don't bear grudges.**❞**

HARRY REDKNAPP

assesses errant midfielder David Bentley

❝I suppose that will be my epitaph at Spurs: he was always talking about injuries. **❞**

GERRY FRANCIS

1997

❝The day I got married, Teddy Sheringham asked for a transfer. I spent my honeymoon in a hotel room with a fax machine trying to sign a replacement. ❞

GERRY FRANCIS

on the stresses he faced at White Hart Lane in the summer of 1997

> **"**I'm amazed he wasn't put on
> his bike at the end of last season.
> After another four months of mid-summer
> muddle, does anyone at Spurs still believe
> he's the business?**"**

DAVID MELLOR

on Christian Gross, August 1998

" Whether you think he's (Harry Redknapp) a top geezer, lovely jubbly man of the people; a shifty, underhand dealing crafty chancer; or simply a melting waxwork of his son Jamie, most people can muster up feelings one way or another for him. West Ham fans love him, Southampton fans hate him. Bournemouth fans love him, Portsmouth fans hate him. Tottenham fans love him, Tottenham fans hate him. **"**

A **FAN**

opines on Footballfancast.com

**❝The trouble with Christian Gross
is that no one had heard of him.
The communication was not brilliant
and I decided, as captain, to explain to him
how things worked and what players liked
and were used to. I do not believe he
listened to a word I said.❞**

GARY MABBUTT

1999

“Someone asked me the other day if I would be tempted if a big job came along in London. My answer is that I have taken on this big job at Leeds and will finish it. **”**

GEORGE GRAHAM

in the Leeds United programme, 1997. The following year he joined Spurs

❝ Short of Margaret Thatcher joining New Labour, it's hard to imagine a more stunning move than Graham going to Spurs. **❞**

DAVID MELLOR

1998

"All that stuff about the Spurs tradition for attractive football is just a crutch. They haven't been playing like that for ages.**"**

GEORGE GRAHAM

soon after becoming manager, 1998

**"I've changed. It's all attack now…
only kidding."**

GEORGE GRAHAM

after Spurs' 5–2 defeat of Watford, 1999

INTERVIEWER

❝What do you feel you have added to Spurs?❞

GEORGE GRAHAM

❝Me.❞

Verbal cut and thrust in an **INTERVIEW**

after a draw at Middlesbrough, 1999

❝I want a consistent team, not a flash one. When I was at Highbury, the message from White Hart Lane used to be, 'Let Arsenal win things with boring football, we'd rather play entertainingly and lose.' I want my team to be exciting, and to win week in, week out. I'm working on it.**❞**

GEORGE GRAHAM

2000

❝He's a coward who will not stand up and admit mistakes. I got mugged into believing that this Adonis of the football world was the be-all and end-all in management skill and tactics. In my time at Tottenham I made lots of mistakes. The biggest was possibly employing him.**❞**

ALAN SUGAR

on George Graham, 2001

"I thought I had seen it all when
it comes to the fickleness of football folk.
Then I heard the Spurs fans singing, 'There's
only one Alan Sugar.'**"**

MICK McCARTHY

Millwall manager, 1994

"To be fair to Tottenham, they tried everything to get Sol round the table to discuss his contract, but he didn't want to talk. People say, why didn't you sell him? But he wouldn't go.**"**

GEORGE GRAHAM

2002

"I don't think I'm the big bad wolf. I can't produce the money to buy players.**"**

DAVID PLEAT

defends Spurs' record in the transfer market, 2003

❝No one at Tottenham would shed a single tear if Glenn Hoddle was sacked tomorrow. The only way they will bring success back to Tottenham is through a change of manager.**❞**

TIM SHERWOOD

May 2003

" There was certainly discontent
in the dressing room. Everyone knows
about his man-management skills –
or lack of them. **"**

NEIL SULLIVAN

on Glenn Hoddle's managerial reign, September 2003

❝The position [Pleat] holds at the club is making it enormously difficult for a manager to succeed. The job will be made just as difficult for any new manager coming in; he should have the job on his own. Let him take on the responsibility and, without his disruptive intervention, the fans might just get their success.**❞**

GLENN HODDLE

2003

" Because of his pride, Hoddle wanted to be the best player in training every day – at 46 years of age. I don't think you can see the whole picture when you're training out there among the guys. Can you imagine Arsène Wenger playing with Thierry Henry and the rest? **"**

DAVID PLEAT

2003

"Glenn Hoddle, if he was singing. **"**

LES FERDINAND

*nominates his ex-Spurs boss as the person he'd least like
to be stuck in a lift with*

" Our central defenders, Doherty and Anthony Gardner, were fantastic and I told them that when they go to bed tonight they should think of each other. **"**

DAVID PLEAT

2004

❝ You don't have to bare your teeth to prove you're a he-man in football. Some people are morally brave – Hoddle is one of them. I've heard him criticised for non-involvement, but if you can compensate with more skill in one foot than most players have in their whole body, then that is compensation enough. **❞**

BRIAN CLOUGH

on Glenn Hoddle the player

❝Hello, my name is Jacques. I am fifty-three years old and I live in London.**❞**

JACQUES SANTINI

introduces himself to the Spurs squad, July 2004

❝ There's no problem with Jermain.
I wouldn't swap him for Miss World –
he would probably swap me for
Miss World though. **❞**

MARTIN JOL

on rumours of a row with Jermain Defoe in 2006

" The first I knew was when I saw my nephew in the tunnel immediately after the game and he pulled me to one side and told me what everyone else seemed to know already. **"**

MARTIN JOL

reveals Spurs' unorthodox methods of getting rid of managers, October 2007

The English league has always been my dream and coaching in England is the realisation of that dream.

JUANDE RAMOS

on becoming Tottenham's manager in October 2007

“He's a little bit naughty. I like how he is because you need to be a little bit naughty when you play football.**”**

Manager **MAURICIO POCHETTINO**

on Dele Alli, 2016

❝He has recommended Juande Ramos, clearly he will have [to take] responsibility if it doesn't work.**❞**

Going. Spurs Chairman **DANIEL LEVY**
reveals the contents of his crystal ball, August 2007

“We have spent around £175m on new players over the last three years… Following a meeting of the directors and a full review of our football management structure, I can inform you that Damien Comolli has left the club with immediate effect.**”**

Gone. **DANIEL LEVY**
confirms that Comolli follows Ramos out of the White Hart Lane door,
October 2008

❝ On the training pitch I speak English and the players understand me perfectly. **❞**

JUANDE RAMOS

insists there is no language barrier between him and the Spurs players

❝To be here, or not to be – that is the question. Do I want to sign a new contract? Why not? But I signed a five-year contract and there are still three years left.**❞**

MAURICIO POCHETTINO

2016

" Tottenham has the potential to improve and be better in the future – a new stadium, an unbelievable training centre, an unbelievable academy, good staff and people. **"**

MAURICIO POCHETTINO

2016

"How the f**king hell did he miss that? My missus could have scored that… You keep pussyfooting around with people – what am I supposed to say? Really good try? Really unlucky? He's really done his best with that?**"**

HARRY REDKNAPP

after Bent heads wide of an open goal from five yards out against Portsmouth, January 2009. Still a Harry fan, Darren?

❝I must admit myself I think I made a mistake… I did cane them a bit and it's not really the way I manage. I get more out of the players by telling them what they can do rather than what they can't do. That has always been my way. **❞**

Four months later, **HARRY REDKNAPP**
apologises to Darren Bent. Sort of…

❝I just told him to tell [Roman Pavlyuchenko] to f**king run around a bit. The boy himself just kept nodding his head. He might be thinking inside: 'What's this t*sser saying to me?'**❞**

Either way **HARRY'S**
conversation with the Russian striker's interpreter seemed to do the trick after he scored the winner against Liverpool, November 2008

"I'll implement a strong rule
next season that drinking is a no-no here.
Footballers should dedicate their lives to
playing. Footballers should not drink. You
shouldn't put diesel in a Ferrari. I know it's
hard but they are earning big money, they
are role models to kids. **"**

HARRY REDKNAPP

puts his foot down after a Ledley King bender makes the front pages, May 2009

❝When you sign a contract as a player, you need to understand that you don't sign to play, you sign to train. Then the club signs a manager or head coach to pick the players. This is football.**❞**

MAURICIO POCHETTINO

2015

"Of course it's pressure, but I am not scared about that. It is something I think I can deal with.**"**

TIM SHERWOOD

starts his managerial career, January 2014

❝I only show emotion at home,
and in my bed. **❞**

MAURICIO POCHETTINO

2014

"It's a massive change and
I admire any manager who gets up there on
the sidelines. I didn't realise you can't sleep
for more than two hours in this job. You wake
up thinking about footballers.**"**

TIM SHERWOOD

gets to grips with his new life as Spurs boss, December 2013

“Tottenham Hotspur has a huge following across the world and I have great admiration for the passion the fans show for this team. We are determined to give the supporters the kind of attacking football and success that we are all looking to achieve.**”**

MAURICIO POCHETTINO

2014

❝He knows the people he works for want Champions League football. If he doesn't get it he's going to be under the cosh. He could be a fantastic manager for Tottenham though… Why not stick with a young English boy who's come through [the ranks]?**❞**

HARRY REDKNAPP

backs Tim Sherwood to stay as Spurs boss, February 2014

CHAPTER 6

IT'S GREAT TO BE A LILYWHITE

❝I love Spurs more than I love football. Unless a match has any real interest concerning Spurs – like Arsenal, who I would always want to lose, every time without question – then there is no link for me. I am first and foremost a Spurs fan, and then a football fan.**❞**

DANIEL STERN

Spurs season-ticket holder and shareholder, 1996

" Even now, when I go over to my mother's house and dig out some of the old tracksuit tops I wore, it makes the hair stand up on the back of my neck. I like to think I am part of a special family. I am no longer connected with the club on a daily basis, but I'm delighted with every win and sad about every defeat. **"**

STEVE PERRYMAN

former captain, 2001

ffThe people who support other
teams don't like me or the way
I play, but that pleases me because if the
Tottenham fans are happy then I have done
well. If the papers say other fans don't like
me, then good, I have done my job.**JJ**

STEFFEN FREUND

2000

162

"At the moment, Spurs are not talked about as a big club, and they are a big club. They demand success and, if you don't give that to a club like Tottenham, the fans complain.**"**

LES FERDINAND

1997

❝The Spurs fans, marching and shouting their way back to the station, banged on the windows of the [team] coach as it threaded its way through the crowds. 'Go on, smash the town up,' said Cyril [Knowles], encouraging them.**❞**

HUNTER DAVIES
author of The Glory Game, *1972*

❝He only puts in guys who work very hard. A lot of guys have left the club. If you do not follow the path, you don't belong in Tottenham.**❞**

Defender **TOBY ALDERWEIRELD**
on manager Mauricio Pochettino, 2016

INTERVIEWER

Which do you you prefer,
Rangers or Celtic?

ALFIE CONN
Spurs

IT'S ONLY A GAME

TV documentary, 1986. Conn played for all three clubs

"I fell in love with the club and it is still my favourite. I was made very welcome there by everyone and the fans were always marvellous. There is always a place in my heart for Tottingham Hotspurs.**"**

OSSIE ARDILES

2000

"We would be perfect for the club. We'd love to. Osvaldo already had a coaching experience there and I'd be eager to do it. It would be a great challenge.**"**

RICKY VILLA

assistant manager to Ossie Ardiles at Argentina's Racing Club,
on managing Spurs, 2003

❝My brother was a West Ham fan.
He took me to Upton Park, but when I came
to my senses at the age of about 12,
I became a Tottenham fan!**❞**

TEDDY SHERINGHAM

2002

" I'm really looking forward to the future and that's what makes it so easy to want to stay here – the fantastic manager we have, the great club, the fans, all the infrastructure we have, the new stadium being built – it's all really exciting and I want to grow with the club at the same pace. **"**

England international **ERIC DIER**

2016

❝My team used to be Tottenham Hotspur, because I liked the way they played the game. They always used to play entertaining football and would attack all the time. They had some great players like Glenn Hoddle and Ossie Ardiles. **❞**

BRIAN LARA

legendary West Indian batsman, 2001

“I'd love to stay here. The club is in great shape at the moment, and we're going forward as a club, and that's important. I'd love to stay for the rest of my career.**”**

Striker **HARRY KANE**

2016

❝I have had six very happy years at Tottenham but it's the right time to say goodbye. We've had some special times together and I've loved every minute of it. Tottenham will always be in my heart.**❞**

GARETH BALE

leaves for Real Madrid, September 2013

❝I want to win things with Spurs.
The League will take a little bit of time,
but we're working towards it. How short are
Spurs of a Championship-winning squad?
Oh God, I don't know. **❞**

STEPHEN CARR

2001

❝I miss playing in England, and I'm not just being polite. The attitude of our coach, Giovanni Trapattoni, is that if we score we must defend immediately. You could say he is the opposite of Ossie Ardiles.**❞**

JURGEN KLINSMANN

at Bayern Munich, before returning to Spurs, 1997

 Taxi For Maicon!

FANS' CHANT

*as Gareth Bale torments Inter's Maicon during Spurs' 3–1 win in the
Champions League, November 2010.*

"I am very happy and excited to have joined Spurs. It's a huge pleasure for my career to be at a club as big as Tottenham. I know it will be a huge challenge but I think I can help all my colleagues to succeed and give a lot of happiness to the supporters.**"**

PAULINHO

says all the right things in the summer of 2013

CHAPTER 7

MAGIC MOMENTS

REPORTER

“Is Klinsmann Spurs'
biggest-ever signing?**”**

OSSIE ARDILES

“No, I was.**”**

Exchange at a **PRESS CONFERENCE**
to unveil Jurgen Klinsmann, 1994

❝I made Gavin a Spurs fan. It fits: a lot of people who sit in the stadium will be from Essex. I told various people, and the next thing you know, the art department have spent £2,000 in the Tottenham shop, and costume have got me a shirt to wear.**❞**

Gavin and Stacey *star* **MATTHEW HORNE**
reveals how art ended up imitating life

"This is my dream, to get the award. I want to get it a second time, a third time. When I take the award home my family will be crazy like you can't believe. They will be really happy.**"**

South Korean forward **SON HEUNG-MIN**
after becoming the first Asian player to be voted the Premier League Player of the Month, 2016

"We hate you so much, cos we loved you so much.**"**

Another **BANNER**

at White Hart Lane on Sol Campbell's return with Arsenal, November 2001

" For those of you watching in black and white, Spurs are in the yellow strip. **"**

JOHN MOTSON

❝ And in the Cup-winners' Cup, Spurs will play either Eintracht or Frankfurt. **❞**

Newsreader **ALISTAIR BURNETT**
and non-football expert, News At Ten, *1982*

❝I expect the Croats to come out… oh dear, I had better not say fighting, had I?**❞**

PETER SHREEVES

Spurs manager, before a match versus Hajduk Split from war-torn Croatia, 1991

❝Tottenham are trying tonight to become the first London team to win this Cup. The last team to do so was the 1973 Spurs side. **❞**

MIKE INGHAM

BBC Radio Five Live

"… and Tottenham ice their sublime cake with the ridiculous.**"**

PETER DRURY

ITV

MAGIC MOMENTS

There are signs at all vomitory entrances advising that alcohol cannot be taken into the seated area.

The **SPURS PROGRAMME**

leaves everyone confused, 2003

❝If it had missed or gone wide,
I'd have got it from my strikers for
hitting it too hard.**❞**

PAUL ROBINSON

talking about his 80-yard free-kick goal
against Watford in March 2007

"I'm an emotional wreck. I went mad.**"**

DAVID BENTLEY

after scoring his first league goal for Spurs – a 45-yard volley

against Arsenal at The Emirates, October 2008

❝You're just a s**t Chas & Dave!❞

SPURS FANS

assess the musical merits of Manchester City fans
Liam and Noel Gallagher, May 2009